FESTIVAL FUN
for the Early Years

CHRISTMAS
and
EASTER

- Fun activity ideas •
- Photocopiable resources •
- Information on customs and beliefs •

SCHOLASTIC

Jenni Tavener

CREDITS

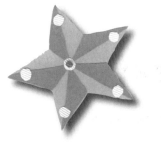

For Chris, Hedley and Leah

Text © Jenni Tavener 2004
© 2004 Scholastic Ltd

Designed using Adobe InDesign

Published by Scholastic Ltd
Villiers House
Clarendon Avenue
Leamington Spa
Warwickshire
CV32 5PR

www.scholastic.co.uk

Printed by Bell and Bain Ltd

4 5 6 7 8 9   6 7 8 9 0 1 2 3

British Library Cataloguing-in-Publication Data
A catalogue record for this book is available from the British Library.

ISBN 0-439-97139-X

Author
Jenni Tavener

Editor
Susan Howard

Assistant Editor
Jennifer Shiels

Series Designer
Catherine Mason

Cover Illustration
Catherine Mason

Illustrations
Bethan Matthews

FESTIVAL FUN CHRISTMAS and EASTER
for the Early Years

CONTENTS

INTRODUCTION

Celebrating festivals with young children

Festivals and celebrations help young children to gain an awareness of their family's culture and traditions. However, children need to be involved in the festival preparations and celebrations at a level that they can understand. Children also need to feel that their contributions are worthwhile. For this reason, the activities in this book involve the children in constructive tasks such as making cards and gifts to send or give to loved ones, creating games to play with others, and making decorations or edible items to share with friends and peers.

Multicultural awareness

Festival celebrations provide good opportunities to help children develop an awareness of different cultures and religions. Many of the customs and traditions associated with the Christian festivals of Christmas and Easter, for example, are very similar to those seen at other religious festivals. Different religions may celebrate different beliefs, stories and historical events, but the ways of celebrating often have common elements, for example, getting together with family and friends, sharing special meals, exchanging gifts, sending cards, decorating places of worship and decorating homes. Like Christmas and Easter, many other festivals also help to remind people of important issues such as kindness, goodness, sharing, love, peace and goodwill to others.

Involving parents in the community

Encourage parents or carers to help organise special events in your setting during each academic year, for example, a festival-themed party, a Christmas fair or an Easter show to raise funds for a local cause. Alternatively, invite the parents and carers to attend pre-organised events that involve their children, for example, a festival sing-song, a seasonal walk, a Nativity play or an Easter parade.

How to use this book

Each festival introduction provides background information such as dates, religious beliefs, customs and traditions. This is followed by a set of poster notes, offering ideas on how to use the two posters with young children, including points to talk about, things to observe and questions to ask. The planning page for each festival shows a topic web that explains how the main activities link up with the six Areas of Learning: Personal, social and emotional development; Communication, language and literacy; Mathematical development, Knowledge and understanding of the world; Physical development and Creative development.

The photocopiable pages include two stories suitable for reading aloud to the children in groups or on a one-to-one basis, and a set of new action rhymes and songs for each festival, all using familiar tunes. There are also seven activity pages for the children to colour, cut and decorate to create items such as an Easter gift bag, a spinner and a seed packet!

Dates

- Advent is the beginning of the church's year. It is the time when Christians prepare for Christmas.
- Advent Sunday is the Sunday nearest to St Andrew's Day on 30 November, and Advent lasts until Christmas Day on 25 December.
- Epiphany follows on 6 January, when the story of the Three Wise Men is remembered.

Religious beliefs

- Christians believe that Jesus is the Son of God and remember his birth at Christmas.
- Christians believe that Jesus was born to bring peace on Earth.
- Christians believe that Jesus helps people to find the good and right way to live.
- Christians believe that Jesus was the Christ, the King of love and peace.
- Christians believe that Jesus' life has helped to brighten up the world with goodness and hope. Jesus is therefore referred to as the 'Light of the World'.

Customs and traditions

- On Advent Sunday, many churches light the first coloured candle on an Advent ring, which is a ring of holly with four coloured candles around the edge and a white candle in the middle. This continues on each of the four Sundays in Advent until Christmas Day, when the white candle is also lit, to symbolise Jesus Christ, the 'Light of the World'.
- Christmas cribs are set up in many churches, schools and homes. They are small models of the stable where Jesus was born and they are displayed to re-mind people of the story of Jesus' birth.
- Christmas Day is a holiday when families try to get together and a traditional Christmas dinner is shared. Meal time traditions are passed down from one generation to the next, such as putting coins in a Christmas pudding for friends or family to find during the meal!
- The popular tradition of decorating a fir tree with brightly coloured objects inside the house was introduced to Great Britain over 100 years ago, by Prince Albert, Queen Victoria's husband.

Celebrations

● Christmas is celebrated in a variety of ways in different countries. One universal celebration is the giving of gifts to children, friends and family. It came about because baby Jesus was given gifts when he was born. The most famous gifts given to Jesus were those from the Three Wise Men of gold (a precious metal), frankincense (a perfume) and myrrh (a medicinal gum).

● Many countries have their own special gift-giving traditions. For example, in Great Britain many children hang out a stocking on Christmas Eve, in the hope that Father Christmas will fill it with presents for them to open in the morning. In France, children leave their shoes out for Père Noël to fill with gifts. In Spain, children wait until 6 January before leaving their shoes on the window sill to be filled with sweets or gifts, and in Denmark children usually open their presents after their Christmas meal.

Using the poster

Display the Christmas poster which shows a young child playing with nativity scene characters in front of a large, decorated Christmas tree and a selection of wrapped presents. Ask the children questions such as, 'Can you see baby Jesus', 'Who are the other characters?', 'Can you see any animals?' and so on. Discuss whether the picture was taken before or after Christmas? How can they tell?

Invite the children to model their own nativity scene using Plasticine, clay or play dough. Help them to decorate plain boxes or pieces of paper with seasonal colours, pictures and repeated patterns.

CHRISTMAS FESTIVAL PLANNER

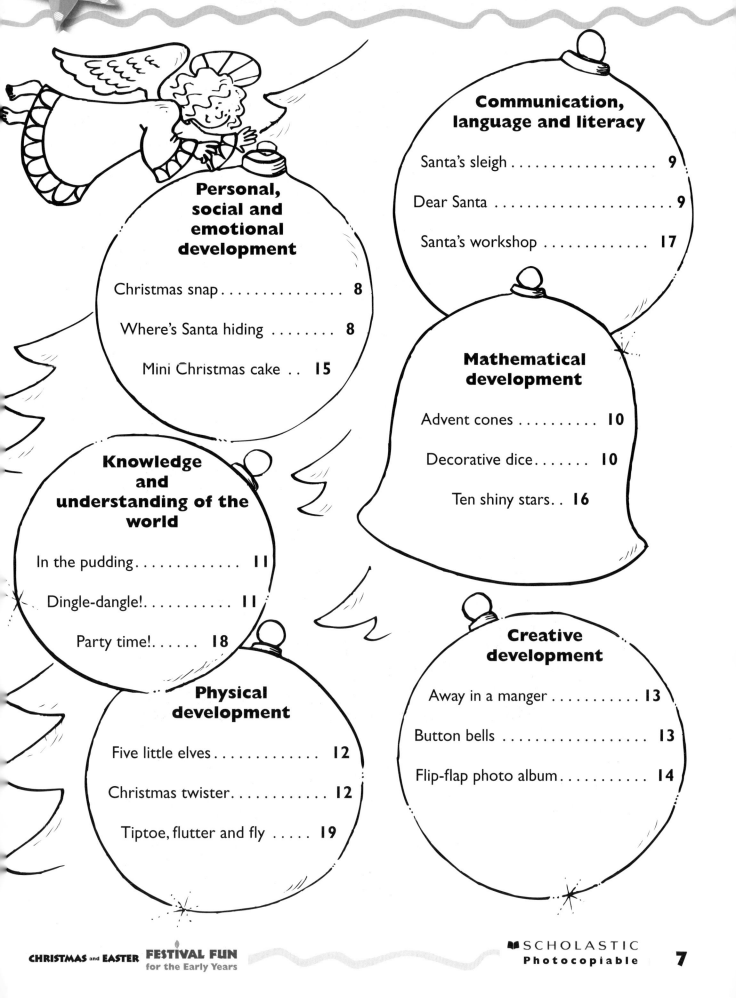

Personal, social and emotional development

CHRISTMAS SNAP

What you need
'Christmas snap' photocopiable sheet on page 23; thin card; safety scissors; pencils or felt-tipped pens.

Preparation
Photocopy the 'Christmas snap' sheet on to thin card so that each child has two copies.

What to do
● Give each child two card copies of the 'Christmas snap' photocopiable sheet, and invite them to colour in the pictures. Help them to cut out the pictures to create a set of 12 playing cards.
● Encourage pairs or small groups of children to use the playing cards to play traditional matching games such as 'Snap' and 'Pairs'.

Early Learning Goal
Work as part of a group or class, taking turns and sharing fairly, understanding that there needs to be agreed values and codes of behaviour for groups of people, including adults and children, to work together harmoniously.

Talk About
Ask the children to identify the six pictures in the set of playing cards. Talk about how each picture links to the theme of Christmas.

WHERE'S SANTA HIDING?

What you need
Four copies of the 'Where's Santa?' photocopiable sheet on page 24 for each child; paints or felt-tipped pens in four different colours; safety scissors; the rhyme 'It's midnight says the clock' on page 21; a large open space where the children can move around freely and safely.

What to do
● Invite the children to use paints or felt-tipped pens in four different colours to decorate the chimney pots on each sheet. For example, the two chimney pots on the first page could be blue, the two pots on the second page could be red, the two pots on the third page could be yellow and the two pots on the fourth page could be green.
● Cut each page in half to create eight separate pictures.
● Position the four pictures showing an empty chimney pot in the four corners of the room. Place the four pictures showing Santa in a pile on the table, face down.
● Invite the children to sing the action rhyme 'It's midnight says the clock' as they skip around the room.
● When they have finished singing, ask the children to guess where they think Santa is hiding by running to one of the coloured chimney pot pictures around the room. Encourage them to sit by their chosen picture.
● When everyone is seated, turn over the top picture from the pile to reveal where Santa is really hiding!
● All the children who are sitting by the same colour chimney have found Santa! Shuffle the pile of cards and play again.

Early Learning Goal
Understand what is right, what is wrong, and why.

Talk About
Encourage the children to talk about their own personal experiences of Christmas.

Further Ideas
● Ask the children to sing and talk about their favourite carols.
● During circle time, provide a Christmas-themed object for the children to pass around, for example, a pretend gift, a shiny star or a baby doll. Use the item as a prompt to encourage the children to share memories, thoughts and feelings about Christmas.
● Help the children to explore the theme of 'giving and receiving' during role-play in the home corner.
● Read the Christmas story on page 20 and discuss issues such as caring, kindness and helping others.

Communication, language and literacy

SANTA'S SLEIGH

Early Learning Goal Use a pencil and hold it effectively to form recognisable letters, most of which are correctly formed.

Talk About Talk with the children about why we give gifts at Christmas.

What you need
'Santa's sleigh' photocopiable sheet on page 25; thin card; the rhyme 'Oh, grand old Santa Claus' on page 21; coloured pencils or felt-tipped pens; safety scissors; glue; small boxes.

Preparation
Photocopy the 'Santa's sleigh' photocopiable sheet on to thin card so that each child has two copies.

What to do
● Give each child two card copies of the 'Santa's sleigh' photocopiable sheet, and invite them to use coloured pencils or felt-tipped pens to follow the handwriting patterns on each sheet.
● Help the children to cut out both pictures and invite them to glue the pictures on to opposite sides of a small box to create a simple 3-D model of a sleigh.
● Encourage the children to imagine that their sleigh is full of presents and to manoeuvre the model up and down while singing the rhyme, 'Oh, grand old Santa Claus'.

DEAR SANTA

Early Learning Goal Know that print carries meaning and, in English, is read from left to right and top to bottom.

Talk About Discuss the importance of saying 'thank you' when somebody gives us a gift.

What you need
'With thanks' photocopiable sheet on page 26; coloured pencils or felt-tipped pens; envelopes.

Preparation
Make an A4 or A3 copy of the photocopiable sheet for each child.

What to do
● Invite the children to talk about the presents that they received at Christmas. Did they have a favourite present?
● Give each child a copy of the photocopiable sheet and help them to read the words.
● Invite the children to write a 'thank you' letter by filling in the spaces on the sheet. Ask younger children to draw a picture of their favourite gift in the box, ask older children to write a short message in the box.
● Encourage the children to colour in the pictures around the border and to place their letter in an envelope to give or send to the appropriate person. Help the children to write the name of the person on the envelope.

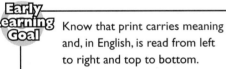
Further Ideas
● Encourage the children to make their own wrapping paper by using festive colours such as red, gold and green to write seasonal words on to a large sheet of paper.
● Read *The Jolly Christmas Postman* by Janet and Allan Ahlberg (Heinemann) to the children.
● Set up a writing table where the children can practise writing Christmas cards and labelling envelopes.
● Help the children to create a seasonal poem by repeating the phrase, 'Red is the colour of…'. For example, 'Red is the colour of Santa's hat. Red is the colour of holly berries' and so on.

Mathematical development

Say and use number names in order in familiar contexts.

Talk About

Talk about Advent calendars with the children. Does anyone have an Advent calendar at home? Invite the children to take it in turns to select a sweet from the Advent cones each day.

ADVENT CONES

What you need

Safety scissors; 25 circles of card (approximately 15cm in diameter); lengths of coloured wool (approximately 10cm long); beads; stapler (adult use); a sturdy branch secured into a bucket of soil or plaster; wrapped sweets; felt-tipped pens.

What to do

● Encourage the children to thread and tie a bead on to the end of each strand of wool. Knot several strands of wool together.

● Invite the children to decorate the circles of card before helping them to cut out a 'v'-shaped section from each circle of card. Insert

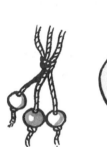

the knot of wool into the centre of the 'v' shape and twist the circle of card to create a cone (see illustration). An adult should staple the cone together.

● Encourage the children to tape a wool handle on to the rim of each cone. Let them watch as you label the cones from 1 to 25.

● Invite the children to put a sweet into each cone and then to hang the cones on a branch to create a 3-D Advent calendar.

DECORATIVE DICE

Early Learning Goal

Use developing mathematical ideas and methods to solve practical problems.

Talk About

Invite the children to discuss alternative rules for your Christmas dice game.

Further Ideas

● Help the children to decorate a paper Christmas tree with repeating patterns.

● Help the children to wrap a variety of different-sized boxes to represent presents. Use the boxes to encourage an awareness of size order and to help develop mathematical language such as 'big', 'bigger', 'biggest', 'smaller than' and 'taller'.

What you need

Empty cube-shaped box; 21 white self-adhesive labels; 20 sheets of paper (approximately 10cm by 10cm); masking tape; felt-tipped pens; a Christmas stocking filled with pretend gifts.

What to do

● Encourage the children to decorate the 21 white sticky labels to represent presents.

● Stick 1 to 6 labels on to the sides of an empty box to create a giant dice. Next, help the children to write the numbers 1 to 20 on to 20 sheets of paper. Tape them in a line on the floor, in numerical order. Place the Christmas stocking at the end of the number track.

● Encourage the children to take turns to throw the dice and help them to go forwards along the track the correct number of moves. The first player to reach the stocking is the winner. Alternatively, you could just play for fun.

CROSS-CURRICULAR IDEAS

Knowledge and understanding of the world

IN THE PUDDING

What you need
Two circles of brown card for each child (approximately 25cm in diameter); felt-tipped pens in shades of light and dark brown; yellow paint; green and red paper; safety scissors; PVA glue; chocolate coins.

What to do
● Invite each child to decorate two circles of card to represent Christmas puddings. Use the brown felt-tipped pens to illustrate pieces of dried fruit, yellow paint to create the effect of dripping custard, and green and red paper to represent sprigs of holly and red berries!
● Help the children to secure the two puddings back to back by placing glue around the outer edge. Leave a small gap in the top to create a pocket.
● When dry, invite the children to slot chocolate coins into the middle of the two puddings. Add a 'Happy Christmas' tag using the left-over red and green paper to create an unusual Christmas card.

Early Learning Goal
Select the tools and techniques they need to shape, assemble and join materials they are using.

Talk About
Tell the children about the tradition of putting coins in a Christmas pudding (see 'Background information and planning' on page 5). Invite them to talk about other Christmas traditions that they know of.

DINGLE-DANGLE!

What you need
Copy of the rhyme 'Snow come down' on page 21; cardboard tubes; strips of light blue paper (approximately 10cm wide and long enough to fit around the cardboard tube); safety scissors; white paint; dark blue felt-tipped pens; PVA glue.

What to do
● Invite the children to create a Christmas decoration based on the words in the rhyme 'Snow come down'.
● Give each child four strips of light blue paper. Encourage them to draw blue raindrops using a felt-tipped pen on one side of each strip and to paint white snowflakes on the other side.
● When the paint is dry, help the children to cut a fringe along all four strips of paper.
● Help the children to glue the four fringes, one beneath the other, on to a cardboard tube (see illustration).
● Invite the children to turn the tube upside down to reveal snowflakes, and back again to show the raindrops. Hang several decorations together to create a seasonal mobile.

Early Learning Goal
Build and construct with a wide range of objects, selecting appropriate resources, and adapting their work where necessary.

Talk About
Invite the children to talk about the type of weather that is typical at Christmas. Encourage them to recall seasonal activities such as building snowmen or collecting icicles.

Further Ideas
● Compare the traditions associated with Christmas to other winter festivals such as Hanukkah, Ramadan and Hogmanay.
● Compare Christmas traditions in other countries. For example, gifts are exchanged on different dates in different countries.

CROSS-CURRICULAR IDEAS

Physical development

Travel around, under, over and through balancing and climbing equipment.

Talk About
Discuss Christmas in other countries around the world. Ask the children to imagine Christmas in the sunshine.

FIVE LITTLE ELVES

What you need
The song 'Five little elves' on page 22; cassette recorder; blank cassette; large open space where the children can move freely and safely.

What to do
● Set up the cassette recorder and record the children singing the song 'Five little elves'.
● Play back the song and as the children listen, encourage them to use movement and mime to recreate the actions of the elves, for example, dancing around and pretending to climb under and over the workshop shelves, trying to balance and then falling off the shelves!

CHRISTMAS TWISTER

Early Learning Goal
Show awareness of space, of themselves and of others.

Talk About
Encourage the children to express feelings of excitement as they anticipate Christmas.

What you need
Large sheet of fabric or card (approximately A1 size); thick felt-tipped pens or fabric pens; masking tape; old wooden brick; five self-adhesive labels.

What to do
● Draw a five by five grid on to the large sheet of card or fabric so that you have 25 squares.
● Help the children to draw 25 shapes on to the grid: five squares, five triangles, five oblongs, five circles and five stars.
● Invite the children to decorate each shape to create 25 simple Christmas pictures, for example, square presents, Santa's triangular hat, oblong Christmas crackers, round puddings and colourful stars.
● Help the children to draw one of these pictures on to each sticky labels. Stick the labels to the brick to make a dice (one side should be left blank).

Further Ideas
● Encourage the children to mime the actions of the reindeer as they swoop through the clouds, slide along rooftops and gallop over hills.
● Use the home corner for role-play situations about Christmas Eve.
● Help the children to create a model of Father Christmas, the sleigh or a reindeer using a malleable material such as clay or play dough.
● Mime the actions of Father Christmas as he fills a sack with toys, climbs in his sleigh, falls down chimney pots, struggles through windows and tiptoes across quiet rooms.

● Now play your own version of Christmas twister! Ask two children to take turns to throw the dice while another two children stand on the grid. After each roll of the dice, ask the children who rolled the dice to say what picture they have rolled, and let the children on the grid move their hands or feet to the corresponding picture square.

CROSS-CURRICULAR IDEAS

Creative development

AWAY IN A MANGER

Early Learning Goal Explore colour, texture, shape, form and space in two or three dimensions.

Talk About Compare your own stable scene to the Christmas story. What other characters could you add?

What you need
'The Christmas story' photocopiable sheet on page 20; low level display board; collage materials such as fabric, tissue and card; PVA glue; paper; safety scissors; brown and blue paint; straw; baby doll; toy crib.

What to do
● Read 'The Christmas story' to the children. When you have finished, talk about stable scene. What sort of animal normally lives in a stable?
● Help the children to draw large, bold outlines of animal faces (such as cows, horses, sheep and pigs) on to paper and cut them out.
● Encourage the children to decorate the outlines with collage materials.
● Help the children to paint the bottom half of a display board to represent an old wooden fence and the top to represent the night sky.
● Invite the children to cut out a large shiny star for the sky and to glue the animal faces along the top of the fence.
● Scatter straw on the floor beneath the display and place the baby doll in the crib on the straw to create your own stable scene.

BUTTON BELLS

Early Learning Goal Explore colour, texture, shape, form and space in two or three dimensions.

Talk About Encourage the children to describe the clothes that are worn by Father Christmas.

What you need
Flat buttons and beads in a variety of colours, shapes and sizes; bell-shaped pieces of card (approximately 8cm by 4cm); PVA glue; Velcro; sticky tape; tinsel; felt-tipped pens.

What to do
● Tell the children that you are going to make Christmas badges. Give each child a bell-shaped piece of card and invite them to decorate it using colourful beads and buttons.
● When the glue has dried, invite the children to decorate the spaces in between the buttons and beads using felt-tipped pens.
● Help the children to tape a small length of tinsel to the top of the bell and a strip of Velcro on the back. Enjoy wearing your festive Christmas badges!

Further Ideas
● Invite the children to draw Christmas scenes using thick black pens. Photocopy the designs to create Christmas cards for the children to colour in or sell at a Christmas fair.
● Make some Christmas tree mobiles by cutting out felt shapes such as stockings, stars and trees, and decorating them with sequins.
● Invite the children to play percussion instruments as they sing their favourite Christmas songs.
● Help the children to construct models of Father Christmas or a snowman using cardboard tubes and collage materials.

Creative development

FLIP-FLAP PHOTO ALBUM

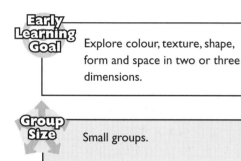

Early Learning Goal

Explore colour, texture, shape, form and space in two or three dimensions.

Group Size

Small groups.

Support and Extension

Help younger children to tape the ribbon in place and tie the knots. Encourage older children to write a message on one of the squares, for example, 'Happy Christmas' or 'Seasons greetings'.

Further Ideas

● Invite the children to cut out 12 pictures from a magazine to create a themed picture album. The theme could reflect the recipient's interests, such as flowers, football, animals or food!

● Divide a small calendar into 12 sections from January to December. Invite the children to use the 12 sections to create a 'flip-flap calendar' to give as a Christmas or New Year gift.

● Help the children to make a 'Thank you' flip-flap booklet to give as a Christmas gift for someone special. Write 'Thank you for' on the first page, followed by appropriate pictures or words on the following pages, for example, 'loving me', 'helping me' or 'being my mummy'.

● Invite the children to draw a seasonal picture on to a sheet of A4 paper using a black pen. Photocopy one picture for each family member. Ask the children to colour in the set of pictures. Laminate them to create a gift set of festive place mats.

What you need

For each child: 12 squares of coloured card (approximately 10cm by 10cm); two lengths of ribbon (approximately 70cm long); masking tape; 12 family photographs taken at Christmas or 12 Christmas pictures cut from magazines; PVA glue; large bead.

What to do

● Give each child 12 card squares. Ask them to place six squares of card in a row, about 1cm apart.

● Help each child to tape two lengths of ribbon across all six squares, then to glue the other six squares on top of the first six, to cover the ribbon (see illustration).

● Encourage the children to trim 12 photographs or pictures to size and to glue them on to the front and back of all six squares.

● Help each child to tie a knot in the ribbon at one end to create a loop, and to thread a large bead on to the ribbon at the other end (see illustration).

● Fold up the photo albums, concertina style, and keep them closed by pushing the bead through the loop.

● Encourage the children to give their Christmas photo album to someone special as a gift.

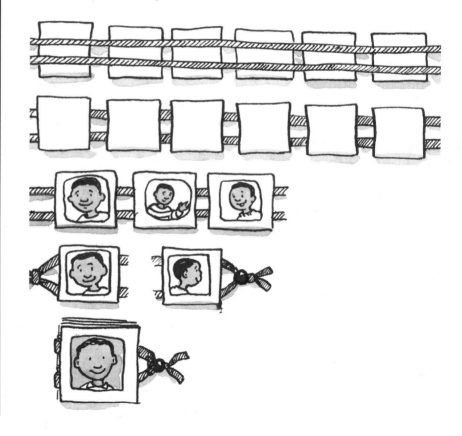

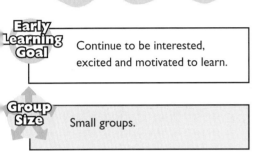

Personal, social and emotional development

MINI CHRISTMAS CAKE

What you need
Hand-washing facilities; aprons; small Christmas cake decorations; wide seasonal ribbon; foil containers lined with greaseproof paper; mixing bowl; wooden spoon; sieve; teaspoon; tablespoon; pastry cutters (the same diameter as the foil containers); cocktail sticks; wire cooling rack.

Ingredients for the cake: 200g self-raising flour; 100g butter/margarine; 100g brown sugar; 100g mixed dried fruit (currants, sultanas or seedless raisins); 1 tsp lemon rind; 1 egg; 5 tbsp milk.

Topping: apricot jam; marzipan; ready-made icing sugar.

Preparation
Check for food allergies before the activity. Encourage the children to wash their hands, tie back long hair and put on clean aprons. If necessary, smooth out the sides of the foil containers to create the shape of mini cake tins.

What to do
● Provide extra adult help as you follow the cake recipe together:

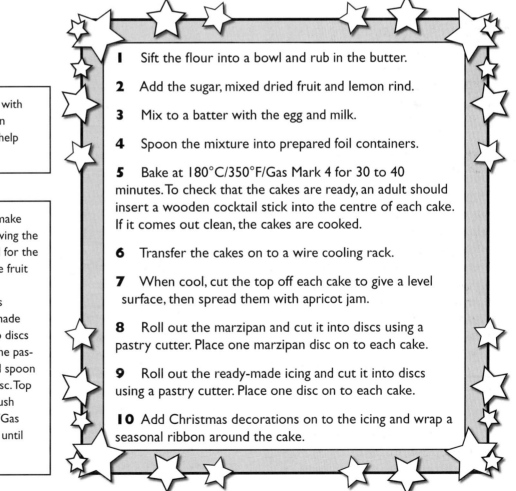

1   Sift the flour into a bowl and rub in the butter.

2   Add the sugar, mixed dried fruit and lemon rind.

3   Mix to a batter with the egg and milk.

4   Spoon the mixture into prepared foil containers.

5   Bake at 180°C/350°F/Gas Mark 4 for 30 to 40 minutes. To check that the cakes are ready, an adult should insert a wooden cocktail stick into the centre of each cake. If it comes out clean, the cakes are cooked.

6   Transfer the cakes on to a wire cooling rack.

7   When cool, cut the top off each cake to give a level surface, then spread them with apricot jam.

8   Roll out the marzipan and cut it into discs using a pastry cutter. Place one marzipan disc on to each cake.

9   Roll out the ready-made icing and cut it into discs using a pastry cutter. Place one disc on to each cake.

10 Add Christmas decorations on to the icing and wrap a seasonal ribbon around the cake.

Mathematical development

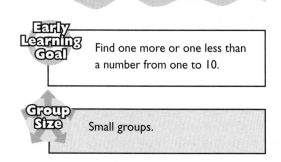

Early Learning Goal
Find one more or one less than a number from one to 10.

Group Size
Small groups.

Support and Extension
Adapt the activity for younger children by singing 'Five shiny stars'. Encourage older children to sing the song by counting down in twos.

Further Ideas

● Label the shiny stars from one to ten, either in numerals or words, and ask the children to remove them from the tree in numerical order as you sing the song.
● Help the children to wrap small 3-D shapes such as cubes, spheres and cylinders to place under the tree in the display. Alternatively, invite the children to hang the shapes on a real tree.
● Create a display based on the traditional Christmas song 'Jingle Bells'. Help the children to cut out several small, medium and large bell shapes from plain paper or card, then decorate the bells using a wide variety of techniques, such as finger painting, collage, printing or glittering. When dry, ask the children to hang a ball of silver foil from the bottom edge of each bell. Cover a display board with all the bells positioned at different angles to represent ringing, jingling bells.

TEN SHINY STARS

What you need
The rhyme 'Ten shiny stars' on page 22; display board at child height covered in a dark backing paper; two sheets of A1 green card; shiny paper or silver foil; glue; safety scissors; red paper; ten small squares of Velcro; ten cardboard star shapes (approximately 10cm by 10cm); sponge shapes; paint in shallow trays.

Preparation
Fold both sheets of green card in half and cut out two symmetrical Christmas tree shapes.

What to do
● Invite the children to sponge print colourful shapes on to one side of the first tree and on to both sides of the second tree.
● When dry, glue or staple the first tree to the backing paper. Create a three-dimensional effect by attaching the second tree on top of the first tree, stapling down the centre fold (see illustration below).

● Give the children the ten star shapes and encourage them to decorate them using pieces of torn shiny paper or silver foil.
● When dry, invite the children to attach the ten shiny stars on to the three-dimensional tree using small pieces of Velcro.
● Sing the song 'Ten shiny stars' with the children and invite them to remove the stars, one at a time, as you sing the song.

Communication, language and literacy

Early Learning Goal
Use language to imagine and recreate roles and experiences.

Group Size
Small groups.

Support and Extension
Encourage younger children to talk about what they are wrapping and to think of imaginary destinations for the toys. Invite older children to write pretend name and address labels for the toys.

Further Ideas
● Help the children to make simple hats using colourful triangles of fabric or paper. Pretend that they are elves' hats, and wear them during role-play.
● Trim two sides of a large cardboard box to make the shape of Santa's sleigh. Invite the children to decorate the outside of the sleigh using paints or collage materials. Place a floor cushion 'seat' and a sack of 'presents' in the sleigh and encourage the children to use it for seasonal role-play scenarios.
● Help the children to paint a fireplace scene, such as a log fire in a brick hearth, on to a large flat cardboard box. Place the fireplace in the home corner and invite the children to decorate the area to represent a Christmas Eve scene.

SANTA'S WORKSHOP

What you need
Home corner or role-play area; low level tables; shelves (or spare tables); containers such as trays, pots and tubs; large blank banner; blank labels; a wide range of colourful gift-wrapping materials (for example, brightly coloured paper, card, tissue, ribbon, bows, shiny thread, wrapping paper); sticky tape; safety scissors; glue; pens; pencils; child-safe hole punch; Christmas cards and posters; Christmas decorations such as streamers and mobiles; toys for wrapping.

Preparation
Ask parents and carers to donate some inexpensive toys.

What to do
● Invite the children to decorate the walls of the role-play area or home corner with Christmas cards, posters, drawings, streamers and mobiles.
● Help the children to write and decorate a large banner saying 'Santa's workshop' to place above the doorway or on the wall.
● Let the children help you to fill several pots, tubs and trays with a wide range of colourful resources suitable for wrapping gifts and making gift tags. Help them to label the containers using bright, bold letters.
● Display the labelled containers in neat rows and create an area to store resources such as glue, scissors and sticky tape.
● Ask the children to display the unwrapped toys in an organised line and to keep an area clear for wrapped toys.
● Label two separate tables with words such as 'Present wrapping' and 'Gift tag making'.
● Invite the children to imagine that they are Santa's helpers or busy elves, and encourage them to join in role-play that involves wrapping gifts and making gift tags.

Knowledge and understanding of the world

Early Learning Goal

Select the tools and techniques they need to shape, assemble and join materials they are using.

Group Size

Small groups.

PARTY TIME!

What you need
Strips of thick card (6cm by 30cm); masking tape; A4 paper; white paper cups; paper crowns or strips of card (10cm by 40cm); old white tablecloth or sheet; green poster paint; red finger paint; wide shallow trays; hand washing facilities; sticky tape; party food.

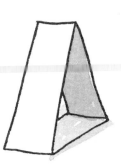
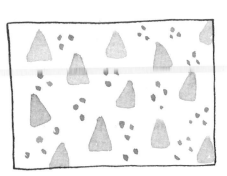

Preparation
Check for food allergies and dietary requirements. Ask parents and carers if they could assist in arranging a Christmas party for the children by donating party food and helping on the day.

What to do
● Help each child to bend a strip of thick card to create a triangle, representing the outline of a Christmas tree. Secure with sticky tape.
● Invite the children to use the tree shape as a printing tool by carefully dipping the edge of the tree into a tray of green paint and then pressing on to a strip of card. Repeat the process several times to create a pattern of Christmas tree shapes. When dry, help each child to bend and tape the card to make a Christmas party hat.
● Encourage the children to use their printing tools to decorate an assortment of paper place mats, paper cups and a tablecloth with random patterns of green tree shapes.
● Provide the children with finger paints to print bright red dots in the spaces between the printed trees. Leave to dry thoroughly and store in a safe place.
● On the day of the party, decorate the tables with the Christmas mats, cups and tablecloth and invite the children to wear their matching party hats.

Support and Extension

Invite older children to help the younger children make the tree-shaped printing tools.

Further Ideas

● Help each child to bend a strip of thick green card to create the outline of a Christmas tree. Thread a red ribbon through each shape to create matching party mobiles.
● Hold a New Year party. Encourage the children to decorate the room with banners, tablecloths, mobiles and posters all showing the words 'Happy New Year' in a variety of colours, sizes and writing styles.

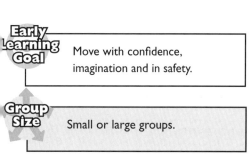

Physical development

TIPTOE, FLUTTER AND FLY

What you need

A5 card templates showing the basic shape of a head and body; child-safe hole punch; thread, strips of thick card (2cm by 10cm); painting and colouring materials; collage materials such as shiny paper, tinsel, wool and netting; glue; Christmas music; large open space where the children can move freely and safely.

What to do

● Give each child an A5 card template showing the shape of a head and body. Help them to make two holes in each side of the body using a child-safe hole punch.

● Provide each child with four strips of thick card to represent two arms and two legs. Help them to punch one hole in the end of each strip of card.

● Help the children to loosely tie the four limbs to the card body using lengths of wool or ribbon to make a puppet (see illustration).

● Now invite the children to decorate both sides of the puppet using pens, pencils or paints to represent a fairy or an elf.

● Use collage materials to add extra features to the elf or fairy, for example, wool or tinsel hair, felt shoes, a fabric hat or net wings.

● Show the children how to twist and turn their puppet to make the limbs flap and dance freely. As they move their puppets, encourage the children to talk about the movements using descriptive words such as 'dangle', 'flutter', 'fly', 'flap', 'jump', 'spin', 'twirl', 'twist' and 'bounce'.

● In a large open space, play some Christmas music and invite the children to mime the movements of their puppet by dancing, twisting, twirling and spinning to the music.

THE CHRISTMAS STORY

Mary was a young woman who lived in a town called Nazareth. Mary was planning to get married to a man called Joseph, who was a carpenter.

One day, an angel came down to visit Mary. The angel told Mary that God had chosen her to have a special child. The angel said that the child would be known as Jesus, the Son of God.

Later on, an angel spoke to Joseph the carpenter. The angel asked him to marry Mary and to look after her. The angel also asked Joseph to help Mary to make a home for Jesus and to bring him up with kindness and love. Joseph agreed.

Mary and Joseph went on a long journey to the town of Bethlehem. Mary sat on a donkey and Joseph led the way. The town of Bethlehem was very busy and bustling with lots of people. Mary and Joseph needed somewhere to stay for the night. But everywhere was full. Eventually, they found a kind innkeeper who said that they could shelter in his stable.

That night, Jesus was born in the stable. Mary wrapped baby Jesus and laid him in a manger so that he could sleep.

Outside, on the hillsides, shepherds were looking after their sheep. An angel came down and told them about Jesus. So the shepherds went to the stable to see the newborn baby.

Sometime later, the Three Wise Men travelled from far away to Bethlehem especially to see the baby. They found their way by following a bright star that was shining in the night sky. They knew that the star would lead them to Jesus. When the Three Wise Men arrived at the stable, they each gave him a gift. One gift was gold, a very precious metal for a precious baby; the second gift was frankincense, a lovely smelling perfume that was also used in places of worship; and the third gift was myrrh, which could be used as a medicine to ease pain.

As the years passed, Jesus grew up into a fine young man who was loved and cared for by Mary and Joseph.

The story of Jesus' life continues in the Easter Story.

Jenni Tavener

It's midnight says the clock

(Sung to the tune of 'Hickory Dickory Dock')

It's midnight says the clock, *(Gesture 12 o'clock with both hands.)*
The reindeer go clip clop, *(Clasp hands together and make clip, clop sound.)*
Santa's coming, to my home, *(Point to yourself.)*
He's filling up my sock! *(Mime pushing presents in a giant Christmas sock.)*

Jenni Tavener

Snow come down

(Sung to the tune of 'Rain, Rain, Go Away')

Rain, rain, go away, *(Wave hand or wag finger.)*
Snow come down so I can play. *(Gesture snow falling with both hands.)*
Rain, rain, go away, *(Repeat first action.)*
Snow come down on Christmas day! *(Repeat second action.)*

Jenni Tavener

Oh, grand old Santa Claus

(Sung to the tune of 'The Grand Old Duke of York')

Oh, grand old Santa Claus, *(Hold arms across an imaginary huge tummy.)*
He had ten thousand gifts, *(Gesture an imaginary huge pile of gifts.)*
He flew them up to the top of the sky, *(Point up.)*
And flew them down again. *(Point down.)*
When they were up, they were up, *(Point up.)*
When they were down, they were down, *(Point down.)*
When they were only half way up, *(Point half way.)*
They were neither up nor down! *(Point up and down.)*

Jenni Tavener

Five little elves

(Sung to the tune of 'Five Speckled Frogs')

Five little happy elves,
Danced around the workshop shelves,
Looking for lots of jobs to do,
Bang, saw!
But one little happy elf,
Fell off the workshop shelf,
Then there were four to bang and saw!
Four little happy elves...
Three little happy elves...
Two little happy elves...
One little happy elf,
Danced around the workshop shelves,
Looking for lots of jobs to do,
Bang, saw!
But this little happy elf,
Fell off the workshop shelf,
Then there were none to bang and saw!

Jenni Tavener

Ten shiny stars

(Sung to the tune of 'Ten Green Bottles')

Ten shiny stars hanging from the tree,
Ten shiny stars hanging from the tree,
But if one shiny star,
Should accidentally fall,
There'll be nine shiny stars hanging on the tree!

Jenni Tavener

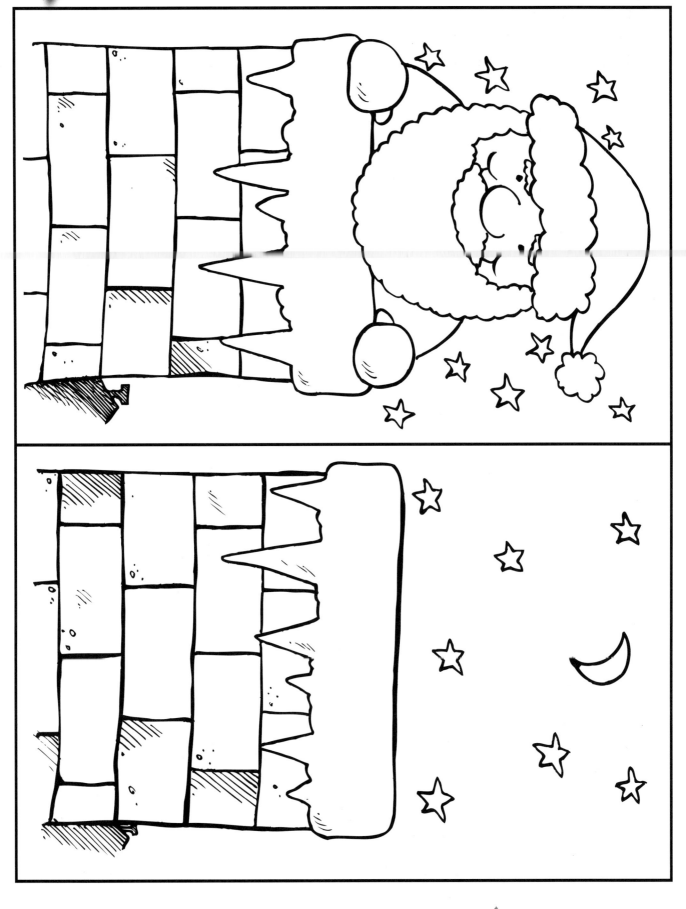

CHRISTMAS
SANTA'S SLEIGH

- Make two copies.
- Start at the dot and follow the arrow.
- Cut out around the dotted edge.

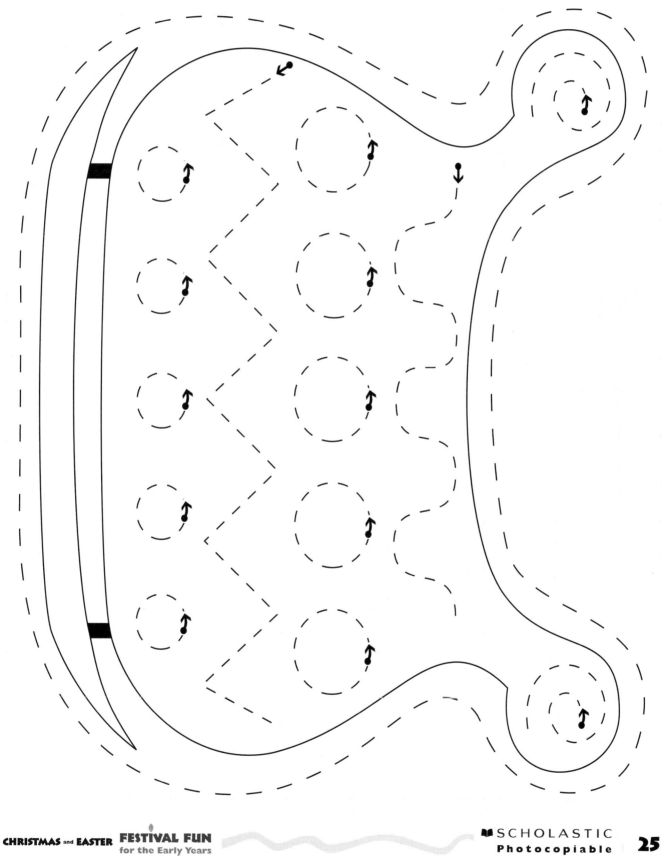

CHRISTMAS
WITH THANKS

Dear

Thank you for the

Love from

FESTIVAL FUN for the Early Years CHRISTMAS and EASTER

BACKGROUND INFORMATION AND PLANNING

Dates

● Easter falls on a different date each year and this can be any time between 21 March and 25 April. It is determined by the Paschal full moon, the first full moon after 21 March.

● Good Friday is the Friday before Easter Day. It is the day when Jesus' crucifixion is remembered.

● Easter Day is always on the Sunday following Good Friday. It is the day when Jesus rose from death.

Religious beliefs

● Christians believe that Jesus died on the cross and forgave others for the very worst things that they could do.

● They believe that Jesus rose from death on Easter Day and that God's love is even stronger than death.

● Christians believe in the teachings and stories told by Jesus, and continue to pass on his good news and messages of love and forgiveness.

● They believe that Jesus is with them in church as they share bread and wine, and during their daily lives as they follow his example.

Customs and traditions

● Easter is the most important festival in the Christian calendar.

● It has become a Christian tradition to eat hot cross buns on Good Friday. The cross on the top of the bun represents the cross at the crucifixion.

● Paschal is an old name for Easter and some people still follow the old custom of lighting a Paschal candle each Easter.

● Easter is a spring festival and many of the customs and traditions link with seasonal events. For example, churches are decorated using spring flowers, leaves and buds, and cards depicting springtime scenes of new life are sent.

● During this festival, children enjoy the tradition of making an Easter garden. This is a small garden scene created in a tray or bowl using as many natural materials as possible. The scene represents the garden where Jesus was seen after his resurrection.

● It has become a tradition for children to take part in Easter bonnet parades. The bonnets are usually home-made and feature seasonal items and natural objects gathered locally, such as flowers, grasses and broken eggshells.

BACKGROUND INFORMATION AND PLANNING

Celebrations

● Easter is celebrated in a variety of ways in different countries. One universal celebration is the giving of Easter eggs to children, friends and family. It is a tradition that has come about because eggs are a symbol of new life. Easter is a festival that focuses on the theme of new life and new beginnings.

● Many countries have their own special Easter egg-giving traditions, for example, in Great Britain many children receive a chocolate egg from each adult in the family. In Germany, adults hide Easter eggs around the house or garden for the children to find and collect. In many other European countries, trees or branches are decorated with small eggs and other symbols of new life, such as spring flowers or small models of spring chicks and lambs.

● The festival of Easter celebrates Jesus' return to life, or resurrection, after his crucifixion on Good Friday. Special church services are held and people rejoice in the 'good news'.

Using the poster

The Easter themed poster shows two chicks nestling on a cracked egg to represent new life and new beginnings. Bright yellow daffodils can be seen in the background to represent the season of Spring. Discuss with the children the traditions associated with Easter and explain why chicks and eggs are often used to represent new life. Ask the children to talk about their favourite Easter celebrations from home.

Invite the children to create their own collage Easter card using real broken eggshells. Encourage them to paint daffodils from first-hand observation, or help them to sew a small soft-toy chick using fake-fur fabric and felt for the beak and eyes.

EASTER
FESTIVAL PLANNER

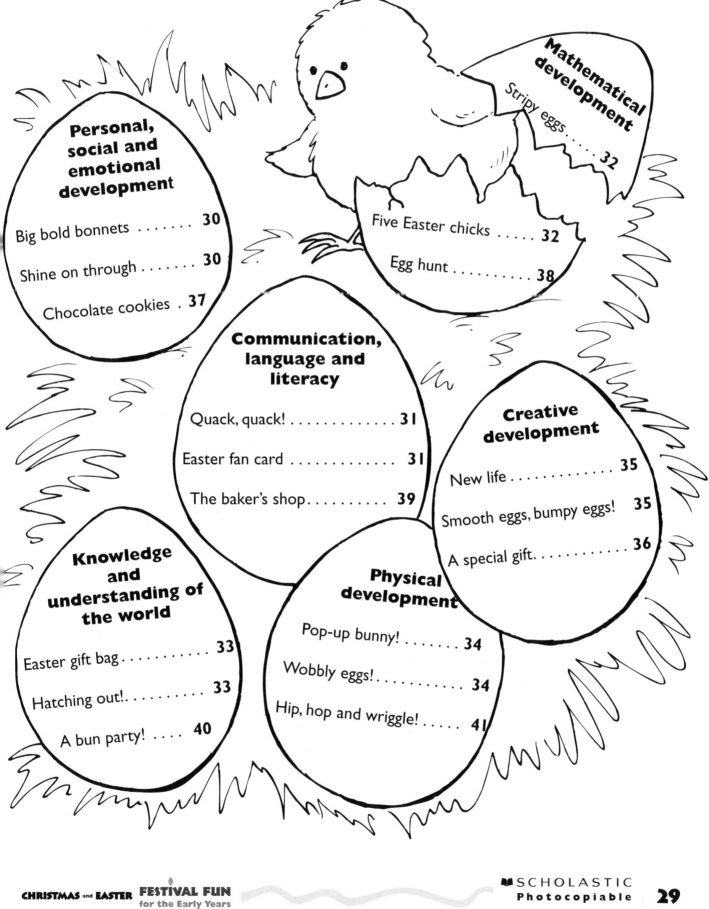

Personal, social and emotional development

BIG BOLD BONNETS

Early Learning Goal
Select and use activities and resources independently.

Talk About
Talk about why spring flowers are often associated with Easter. (See 'Background information and planning' on page 27.)

What you need
The action rhyme 'Sun come out' on page 43; card ovals; felt-tipped pens or collage materials such as sticky paper shapes, tissue, fabric, braid and lace in spring colours; glue; child-safe hole punch; thick ribbon or strips of crêpe paper.

What to do
● Give each child an oval-shaped piece of card. Encourage them to decorate it with spring flowers using felt-tipped pens or collage materials in spring colours.

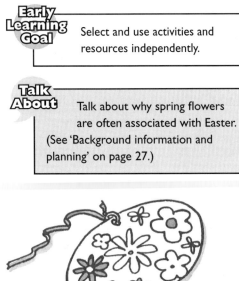

● Tell each child to use a child-safe hole punch to make two holes in opposite sides of the oval.
● Help the children to thread a strip of ribbon or crêpe paper through the holes to create an Easter bonnet (see illustration).
● Invite the children to wear their bonnets as they march together singing the action rhyme 'Sun come out'.
● Alternatively, encourage the children to wear their bonnets for an Easter parade.

SHINE ON THROUGH

Early Learning Goal
Continue to be interested, excited and motivated to learn.

Talk About
Talk to the children about the significance of the cross at Easter. (See 'Background information and planning' on page 27.)

What you need
Squares of white cotton fabric (approximately 25cm by 25cm) for each child; masking tape; thick black permanent pen; felt-tipped pens; cardboard (approximately 30cm by 30cm); sunny window.

What to do
● Give each child a square of cotton fabric and a sheet of cardboard.
● Help the children to use masking tape to secure all four edges of the fabric on to the cardboard. Make sure that the fabric remains taut.
● Encourage each child to use a thick black permanent pen to draw a bold cross in the centre of the fabric.
● Now invite the children to decorate the white fabric around the cross with random patches of colour or patterns using felt-tipped pens. The ink from the felt-tipped pens will spread and merge to create a pretty mottled effect around the cross.
● Ask the children to remove the decorated cotton fabric from the cardboard and tape the fabric on to a sunny window. The sunlight will shine through the material and the felt-tipped pen, creating a stain glass window effect around the black cross.

Further Ideas
● Pass a soft toy such as an Easter chick or lamb around a circle as a prompt to share memories, thoughts and feelings about Easter.
● Encourage the children to sing and talk about an Easter hymn such as 'Lord of the Dance' (from the book *Someone's Singing Lord* published by A & C Black).
● Explore the theme of new life by providing toy animals and accessories such as baskets, blankets and food bowls in the role-play area. Encourage the children to join in role-play based on caring for baby animals.

Communication,
language and literacy

QUACK, QUACK

What you need

A4 card; circles of yellow felt or fake-fur fabric in two different sizes (6cm diameter and 12cm diameter); ovals of yellow felt (8cm by 4cm); PVA glue; orange card cut into small diamond shapes (2cm by 4cm); blue felt-tipped pens.

Preparation

Fold a sheet of A4 card in half for each child.

What to do

● Give each child a folded sheet of card, one small and one large circle of yellow fabric and two ovals of yellow felt.
● Encourage the children to mix and match the four pieces of fabric until they resemble the shape of an Easter chick. Explain that there is no right or wrong way, as there are many variations.
● Help each child to glue the four pieces of fabric, in the chosen position, on to the front of the folded card.
● Give each child a small diamond shape cut from orange card. Help them to fold the orange card in half to represent a beak that opens and shuts. Encourage the children to glue the beak on to their chick.
● Invite the children to draw one or two eyes on to their chick (depending on their chosen design) using a blue felt-tipped pen.
● Help the children to write a simple Easter message inside the card to give to friends or family.

Early Learning Goal
Write their own names and other things such as labels and captions and begin to form simple sentences, sometimes using punctuation.

Talk About
Talk about other pictures that would be suitable for an Easter card, such as a cross or symbols of new life such as baby animals, eggs and spring flowers.

EASTER FAN CARD

What you need

Egg shapes cut from A4 card; felt-tipped pens; paper fasteners; pencils.

What to do

● Give each child five card eggs and help them to write an Easter message by putting one word on to each shape, for example, 'Happy Easter love from (child's name)'.
● Invite the children to decorate the five eggs using different-coloured felt-tipped pens.
● Help the children to secure the eggs together, in the correct order, using a paper fastener. Show them how to open and close the card, like a fan, to reveal the Easter message (see illustration).

Early Learning Goal
Use a pencil and hold it effectively to form recognisable letters, most of which are correctly formed.

Talk About
Talk about the tradition of giving chocolate eggs at Easter. (See 'Background information and planning' on page 28.)

Further Ideas
● Help the children to write the letters 'a' to 'z' on to 26 paper eggs. Display the eggs in alphabetical order to create a colourful letter frieze.

CROSS-CURRICULAR IDEAS

Mathematical development

Early Learning Goal
Talk about, recognise and recreate simple patterns.

Talk About
If possible, show the children a selection of wrapped Easter eggs and encourage them to describe and compare the different patterns.

STRIPY EGGS

What you need
Egg-shaped card (A4 size) for each child; strips of colourful fabric, ribbon or paper; PVA glue; safety scissors.

What to do
● Help the children to make an egg-shaped collage by cutting different lengths of ribbon or fabric and gluing them on to their egg-shaped sheet of card in a pattern of vertical or horizontal stripes.
● Encourage older children to create structured patterns, for example, stripes with alternating colours such as red, blue, red, blue; or repeated patterns such as green, red, yellow, green, red yellow.
● Display the decorated eggs and encourage the children to discuss and compare the different patterns.

FIVE EASTER CHICKS

Early Learning Goal
Say and use number names in order in familiar contexts.

Talk About
Explore the theme of new life by showing and discussing pictures of chicks hatching.

Further Ideas
● Encourage the children to paint five pictures, one for each verse from the song 'Five Easter chicks' on page 44. Help the children to label the pictures 1 to 5. Display the pictures in numerical order or use them to make a counting book.
● Invite the children to model ten eggs using Plasticine or play dough in three different colours. Ask questions such as, 'How many red eggs?' or, 'How many green and yellow eggs?'.
● Help the children to model life-sized eggs using play dough, and place them in plastic egg cups. Ask the children to look away while you remove one or more eggs from the cups. Ask questions such as, 'How many eggs have I taken away?' and, 'How many are left?'.

What you need
The song 'Five Easter chicks' on page 44; five large egg shapes cut from thick coloured card.

What to do
● Hide the five card eggs around the room.
● Ask five children to follow each other around the room to search for an egg while everyone sings: 'Five Easter chicks went searching one day, for an Easter egg to give away. They found an egg that was big and fat, but only four Easter chicks helped carry it back!'.
● Ask four of the children to help carry the card egg back.
● Repeat for the other four verses.

EASTER
CROSS-CURRICULAR IDEAS

Early Learning Goal

Look closely at similarities, differences, patterns and change.

Talk About

Encourage the children to talk about other celebrations that involve giving and receiving gifts.

EASTER GIFT BAG

What you need
'Easter gift bag' photocopiable sheet on page 45; safety scissors; glue; coloured pencils or felt-tipped pens; ribbon; shredded tissue paper; child-safe hole punch; mini Easter eggs.

What to do
● Give each child a copy of the photocopiable sheet. Invite them to colour in the chick and to use a variety of coloured pens or pencils to follow the zigzag handwriting patterns.
● Encourage the children to cut around the thick black line and to use a hole punch to make four holes along the top edge of the picture.
● Help them to change the 2-D picture into a 3-D bag by folding and gluing the two flaps as indicated on the sheet.
● Invite the children to tie a ribbon through the holes to make small handles.
● Provide shredded tissue paper and small wrapped sweets, such as mini Easter eggs, for the children place in the bag as an Easter gift for someone special.

Early Learning Goal

Ask questions about why things happen and how things work.

Talk About

Talk about new life using life cycle examples, such as caterpillar to butterfly, tadpole to frog, and egg to chicken.

Further Ideas

● Make Easter gardens using natural materials such as small stones, twigs, flowers,
● Help the children to match pictures of baby animals to their mothers.
● Discuss the foods that we traditionally associate with Easter, for example, Simnel cake, chocolate nest cakes and hot cross buns.
● Compare the traditions associated with Easter to other spring festivals.

HATCHING OUT!

What you need
'Hatching out' photocopiable sheet on page 46; card; safety scissors; yellow felt-tipped pens; glue; child-safe hole punch; elastic bands.

Preparation
Photocopy the 'Hatching out' sheet on to card so that you have one copy for each child.

What to do
● Give each child a photocopied sheet. Encourage the children to colour the chick in bright yellow and to cut around the dotted line. Help them to fold and glue the two pictures back to back.
● Make a hole in each side of the disc using a hole punch. Thread an elastic band through each hole. To keep the bands in place, thread one end back through its loop.

● Show the children how to twist the elastic bands around and around, then let go! As the disc spins, the chick appears to sit inside the cracked egg!
● Encourage the children to talk about the illusion.

Physical development

POP-UP BUNNY!

What you need
Small plastic yoghurt pots or flower pots with a hole in the base; dowelling; white card circles slightly smaller in diameter than the plastic pots; PVA glue; felt-tipped pens; strong tape such as insulating tape; white felt or fake-fur fabric; safety scissors.

What to do
● Encourage the children to use felt-tipped pens to draw bunny features on to circles of white card.
● Invite the children to cut out two rabbit ears using white felt or fake-fur fabric. Help them to tape the ears and a length of dowelling to the reverse side of the face.
● Ask the children to glue a second circle of white card on to the reverse side of the face to represent the back of the bunny's head.
● Show the children how to fit the dowelling inside the hole in their pot and slide it freely up and down to represent a bunny popping its head out of a flower pot (see illustration).

Early Learning Goal
Use a range of small and large equipment.

Talk About
Discuss why baby animals are often associated with Easter.

WOBBLY EGGS!

What you need
Malleable materials such as clay, play dough or Plasticine; real egg (hard boiled); small ball.

What to do
● Encourage the children to describe the differences between the shape of the egg and the ball.
● Invite them to roll the egg across the floor, and then to roll the small ball. Compare the two.
● Talk about how the shape of the egg affects the way it wobbles as it rolls. Explain that if eggs were round they could roll a long way away from a nest.
● Invite the children to recreate the egg shape and the sphere, using a malleable material such as Plasticine or clay.
● Encourage the children to test the shape of their models by seeing how well they wobble and roll!
● Store the models in open baskets for a 'look and touch' interactive display.
● Extend the activity by inviting the children to model eggs in different sizes.
● Look at pictures (or real examples) of large and small eggs.
● Talk about the different types of birds that lay large and small eggs.

Early Learning Goal
Handle tools, objects, construction and malleable materials safely and with increasing control.

Talk About
Pass a plastic or wooden egg around during circle time. Invite the children to take turns to talk about their favourite Easter time memories or to express thoughts, views and feelings about the Easter story.

Further Ideas
● Encourage the children to mime the actions of a ball or an egg shape by rolling and wobbling around the floor, avoiding others in their path.
● Challenge the children to listen to instructions to help them find a hidden egg.
● Move around imaginatively, pretending to be a chick or lamb.
● Mime the actions to the words in the Easter rhymes 'Tippity, tappity, knock' and 'This poor old Easter egg!' on page 43.
● Invite the children to play games that involve hunting and counting pretend eggs hidden in a sandpit.

CROSS-CURRICULAR IDEAS

Creative development

NEW LIFE

Early Learning Goal
Respond in a variety of ways to what they see, hear, smell, touch and feel.

Talk About
Talk about new life with reference to plant life cycles such as seed to vegetable, bulb to flower, and acorn to tree.

What you need
'Seed packet' photocopiable sheet on page 47; seeds that are easy to grow, such as sunflower or nasturtium; plant pots; soil; water; sunny window sill; safety scissors; glue; pencils.

What to do
● Talk to the children about how Easter represents 'new life'.
● Let each child choose a few seeds. Help them to plant some of the seeds in a plant pot and allow them to save the rest to take home.
● Give each child a copy of the photocopiable sheet and encourage them to cut, fold and glue it where indicated.
● Invite the children to place their spare seeds in their new packet and to draw a picture of a flower on the front to show the seeds they have chosen.
● Help the children to complete the information on the back of the packet by writing or copying their name and the type of seeds in the packet.
● Invite the children to take their seeds home for planting. (Check first with parents and carers that they are willing and able to help their child to plant and care for the seeds at home.)

SMOOTH EGGS, BUMPY EGGS!

Early Learning Goal
Explore colour, texture, shape, form and space in two or three dimensions.

Talk About
Discuss Easter traditions that are popular in other countries. (See 'Background information and planning' on page 28.)

Further Ideas
● Make a shiny egg collage using a selection of foil sweet wrappers.
● Show the children how to use a wide variety of traditional painting techniques to decorate paper egg shapes, for example, splatter painting, marbling, potato printing and finger painting. Use the decorated eggs to make a colourful Easter display.

What you need
Egg-shaped sheets of card, A4 size; poster paint in three different colours; PVA glue; three textured materials such as sand, wood shavings and tissue paper; three large, clean plastic tubs such as empty margarine tubs; old paintbrushes.

What to do
● In three separate tubs, help the children to mix two parts of poster paint with one part of PVA glue. Use one colour of paint in each tub.
● Let the children add sand to one tub, wood shavings to the second tub and tissue paper to the third tub to create three colourful textured mixtures.
● Give each child an egg-shaped sheet of card and invite them to use the mixtures to decorate the card eggs with textured patterns.
● When dry, decorate the top of the card with a silky bow and add a loop for hanging.
● Display the eggs for the children to observe, feel, describe and compare.

EASTER
CRAFT AND GIFT IDEAS

Creative development

A SPECIAL GIFT

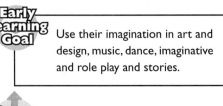

Early Learning Goal
Use their imagination in art and design, music, dance, imaginative and role play and stories.

Group Size
Individuals or small groups.

What you need
Small box for each child; paper (large enough to wrap around box); felt-tipped pens; sticky tape or narrow ribbon; blank labels or gift tags.

Preparation
Write a personalised gift tag for each child showing the following poem: 'This special gift is wrapped up tight. But open, you must never! (Child's name) blew a kiss inside, and sealed the kiss forever. This special gift is wrapped up tight. But open, you must never! (Child's name) wrapped this kiss with love, for you to keep and treasure.'

What to do
● Ask the children to make an Easter gift for someone special.
● Give each child a piece of paper and invite them to use felt-tipped pens to decorate it with colourful symbols of new life and new beginnings, such as flowers, chicks and eggs.
● Next provide the children with a small box. Encourage everyone to open the lid of their box and to blow a kiss inside. Quickly shut the lids and ask the children to imagine that their kiss is sealed inside.
● Help each child to wrap the box using their decorated paper.
● Give each child a gift tag showing a personalised copy of the poem. Read and discuss the poem with the children.
● Encourage the children to draw some kisses around the poem and to stick or tie the tag on to the gift for someone special.

Support and Extension
Help younger children during the wrapping stage. Encourage older children to copy the poem on to the gift tag or to write their own name in the appropriate places.

Further Ideas
● Focus on new life and new beginnings by inviting the children to paint pictures of spring flowers from first-hand observation.
● Add food colouring to marzipan and help the children to model mini egg shapes as sweet gifts to take home.
● Give each child two ovals of yellow felt to sew or glue together. Add toy stuffing, two felt eyes and a felt beak to create a simple soft toy Easter chick. Alternatively, sew or glue two ovals of felt together, leaving a gap in the bottom edge. Decorate as before to create a simple egg cosy.
● Help the children to grow some cress seeds on a sheet of blotting paper cut into the shape of a cross. Let them take the cress home as a gift.

36

COOKERY IDEAS

Personal, social and emotional development

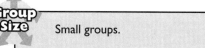

Early Learning Goal

Work as part of a group or class, taking turns and sharing fairly, understanding that there needs to be agreed values and codes of behaviour for groups of people, including adults and children, to work together harmoniously.

Group Size

Small groups.

Support and extension

Invite younger children to decorate the cookie using a random assortment of sweets. Encourage older children to place the sweets in a repeated pattern or a pattern of colours.

Further Ideas

● Explore chocolate-flavoured food and drinks. Help the children to make chocolate milkshake, adding a scoop of chocolate ice-cream to the drink to make a special treat.
● Invite the children to make egg-shaped chocolate spread sandwiches.
● Make fruity treats by dipping strawberries or grapes into a plastic bowl of warm melted chocolate.
● Let the children experience cracking an egg into a small bowl. Use the broken eggs to make a chocolate cake.

CHOCOLATE COOKIES

What you need

Hand-washing facilities; clean aprons; plastic mixing bowls; spoons; forks; baking trays; wire cooling rack; thick white ribbon; felt-tipped pens; self-adhesive labels.

Ingredients: 200g self-raising flour; 25g cocoa powder; 150g butter; 100g caster sugar; beaten egg; pinch of salt; small sweets such as chocolate buttons or dolly mixtures; icing sugar; water.

Preparation

Check for food allergies and dietary requirements. Ask the children to wash their hands, tie back long hair and put on clean aprons.

What to do

Help the children to follow this simple recipe, with an adult helper:

1   Sift the flour, salt and cocoa powder into a bowl and rub in the butter finely.

2   Add the sugar and mix to very stiff dough with the beaten egg.

3   Divide the dough between the children. Ask them to pat the dough, using floured hands, to create a flat egg shape.

4   Transfer the dough on to a buttered baking tray and prick with a fork.

5   Bake in an oven at 180°C/350°F/Gas Mark 4 for about 12 to 15 minutes.

6   Remove the cookies from the oven and leave them on the tray for a couple of minutes before transferring them to a wire cooling rack.

7   Invite the children to mix a thin paste with the icing sugar and water. Use the paste to stick small sweets or chocolate buttons on to their cookie.

● Encourage each child to personalise a length of ribbon using felt-tipped pens. Tie the ribbon around the middle of the cookie.
● Help the children to write a short Easter message such as 'Happy Easter' on to a sticky label to place next to the ribbon.

Mathematical development

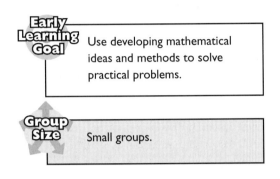

Early Learning Goal
Use developing mathematical ideas and methods to solve practical problems.

Group Size
Small groups.

Support and Extension
Help younger children to create a display that hides 1 to 5 Easter eggs. Ask older children problem-solving questions such as, 'Which two bushes are hiding a total of three Easter eggs?' or, 'Can you find three bushes that are hiding a total of six Easter eggs?'.

Further Ideas
• Invite the children to draw groups of 1 to 10 Easter eggs on to ten sheets of card. Label the pictures 1 to 10 and glue them in numerical order to create an Easter egg numberline.

• Help the children to cut egg shapes from three different colours of paper, for example, red, yellow and blue to create an Easter collage. Use the collage to inspire counting skills by asking questions such as, 'How many red eggs can you see?', 'How many red and blue eggs altogether?', 'How many yellow eggs would there be if one more was added to the collage?'.

• Decorate 15 cardboard eggs on both sides using paints, pastels, crayons or felt-tipped pens. Hang the decorated eggs in groups of 1 to 5 to create five Easter counting mobiles.

EGG HUNT

What you need
Display board at the children's height covered in green backing paper; paints and paintbrushes; ten sheets of green A4 card; ten sheets of A4 paper; safety scissors; strong tape or a staple gun (adult use).

Preparation
Cut a wavy edge around ten sheets of green A4 card to represent the shape of ten bushes.

What to do
● Encourage the children to paint colourful flowers, butterflies, bees, buds and leaves on to the ten sheets of green card to represent ten bushes in springtime.

● When dry, tape or staple the top edge of each picture on to the display board to make ten flaps depicting a garden scene.

● Next, encourage the children to paint groups of 1 to 10 colourful Easter eggs on to the ten sheets of paper.

● When dry, help the children to cut away any excess paper from around each group of eggs.

● Glue one group of eggs under each flap on the display board.

● Use the display to find, count and compare the number of Easter eggs hidden behind each flap by asking questions such as, 'Can you find the bush that is hiding the most Easter eggs?', 'Which bush is hiding the least number of Easter eggs?' or, 'How many eggs can you find altogether under these two bushes?'.

ROLE-PLAY IDEAS

Communication, language and literacy

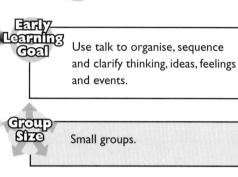

Early Learning Goal
Use talk to organise, sequence and clarify thinking, ideas, feelings and events.

Group Size
Small groups.

Support and Extension
Provide younger children with only 1p coins. Encourage older children to handle 1p, 2p, 5p and 10p coins.

Further Ideas
● Help the children to turn the role-play area or home corner into a chocolate shop or chocolate factory. Invite them to make and decorate pretend chocolates and Easter eggs using brown Plasticine to display and sell in the shop or factory.
● Help the children to set up a farm shop in the role-play area. Share ideas about the type of products they could pretend to 'sell', such as Plasticine eggs, toy fruit and vegetables, resealed empty food packets, or clean pots and tubs with new paper lids and labels.
● Invite the children to create an old fashioned sweet shop with weighing scales, brown paper bags and plastic jars of pretend sweets. Stress that nothing in the shop must be eaten.
● Explore the theme of 'Spring' by helping the children to make pretend plants and flowers for a market stall.

THE BAKER'S SHOP

What you need
Strips of white card; sticky tape; salt dough or another malleable material; tray; role-play area or home corner; white cloth; toy till; real or pretend money; paper bags; blank labels; pens or pencils.

What to do
● Sing the traditional rhyme 'Hot Cross Buns' with the children: 'Hot cross buns, hot cross buns. One a penny, two a penny, hot cross buns. If you have no daughters, give them to your sons. One a penny, two a penny, hot cross buns.'

● Help the children to make a simple headband to represent a baker's hat, using a strip of white card and some sticky tape.
● Invite the children to wear the hat while they make batches of pretend hot cross buns using salt dough or another malleable material. Store the buns on a tray.
● Encourage the children to share ideas, views and feelings about how they can turn the role-play area or home corner into a baker's shop. For example, they could cover a table in a white cloth to display the tray of buns and place a toy till, real or pretend money and paper bags on a second table for purchasing the buns.
● Talk about suitable signs and labels for the shop. Help the children to write or copy price tags and labels saying 'One a penny', 'Two small buns for a penny', 'Open', 'Closed' and 'Lovely hot cross buns for sale'.
● Encourage the children to join in role-play that involves buying and selling the buns for 'one a penny' or 'two a penny'.

Knowledge and understanding of the world

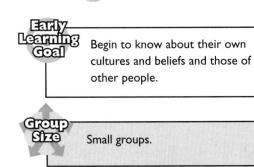

Early Learning Goal
Begin to know about their own cultures and beliefs and those of other people.

Group Size
Small groups.

A BUN PARTY!

What you need
Ingredients to make hot cross buns (see below); hand-washing facilities; clean aprons; butter; two bowls; sieve; teaspoon; tablespoon; baking tray; wire cooling rack; chopping board; blunt knives; plastic plates; colourful paper; felt-tipped pens; table cloths; paper napkins.

Ingredients: 225g plain flour; 25g sugar; 12g fresh yeast (or half a tbsp of dried yeast); 75ml milk; 2 tbsp of warm water; half a tsp of salt; 1 tsp of mixed spice; 50g currants; 25g butter; half a beaten egg.

Preparation
Check for food allergies and dietary requirements. Provide the children with colourful paper and pens, and help them to write or draw a simple 'bun party' invitation to give to a favourite teddy or toy.

What to do
● On the day of the party, invite the children to wash their hands and to put on clean aprons.
● Make some mini hot cross buns using the following recipe:
● Sift 50g of flour into a bowl and add half a tsp of sugar.
● Blend the yeast with milk and water. Add to the flour and sugar.
● Mix well and leave for about 30 minutes or until frothy.
● Meanwhile, sift the remaining flour, salt and spice in another bowl. Add the sugar, currants, butter and half a beaten egg. Mix to a soft dough with the frothy yeast mixture.
● Knead the dough on a floured chopping board for about five minutes.

● Cover and leave to rise until it has doubled in size.
● Knead once more on a floured board and divide into twelve pieces.
● Place well apart on a buttered baking tray and leave to rise once more for about 30 minutes.
● Cut a cross in the top of each bun and bake for about 20 minutes at 220°C/425°F/Gas Mark 7.
● Place on a wire cooling rack.
● When cool, help the children to spread butter on to the buns. Alternatively, use shop-bought buns.
● Ask the children to help decorate the room by placing table cloths, plastic plates and paper napkins on the tables, and seating toys or teddies on spare chairs.
● Hold your own celebration by sharing and eating the hot cross buns with the children.

Support and Extension
Help younger children to wash their hands properly before handling food. Encourage older children to make Easter place mats or name cards for the party.

Further Ideas
● Help the children to make and wear bunny ears for an Easter bunny picnic.
● Find out about the celebrations associated with other spring festivals such as Hanamatsuri, Baisakhi, Passover and Holi.

Physical development

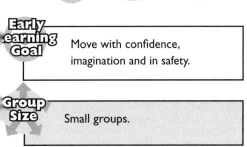

Group Size
Small groups.

HIP, HOP AND WRIGGLE!

What you need
The song 'Hip, hop, wriggle' on page 44; large open space where the children can move freely and safely; strips of white card; white paper or fabric; strong tape; safety scissors.

Preparation
Help each child to make a simple headband using a strip of white card. Encourage them to cut out the shape of two bunny ears using white paper or fabric to attach to the headband. Invite them to wear their bunny ears for the following circle dance.

What to do
● Encourage everyone to stand together in a large circle.
● Sing the song 'Hip, hop, wriggle' with the children to the tune of 'In and Out the Dusty Bluebells'.
● As you sing the words 'In and out jumps the Easter bunny', ask one of the children to pretend to be an Easter bunny by jumping and weaving in and out of the circle, then returning to their original place.
● As you sing 'Let's all jump together', encourage all of the children in the circle to jump on the spot.
● When you get to the words 'Hip, hop, hip, hop, wriggle my tail', invite all of the children to hop on the spot and to wriggle an imaginary bunny tail.
● Finally, as everyone sings the words 'Let's all jump together', encourage everyone to jump on the spot once again.
● Repeat the song several times, inviting a different child to be the Easter bunny each time.

Support and Extension
● Ask an older child to lead a younger child in and out of the circle.

Further Ideas
● Encourage the children to sing the song as they move around the room, free style, imitating the actions of an Easter bunny. Ask them to think of words to describe their movements, for example, 'hopping', 'jumping', 'leaping', 'scurrying', 'digging', 'thumping feet', 'washing ears', 'wriggling tail' and 'twitching whiskers'.
● Focus on two or three of the descriptions to create a sequence of repeated movements, for example, a scurry and a wriggle, or a hop, leap and jump.
● Encourage the children to imitate the movements of other Easter animals, such as a lamb or a chick.
● Play some instrumental music and encourage the children to make up short dance sequences based on the movements of baby animals.

THE EASTER STORY

When Jesus was grown up he became a preacher and a teacher. He helped people to find the good and right way to live. He told them to 'treat others as you would like to be treated yourself', 'to love your enemies' and to 'forgive others if they do wrong to you'.

People said that they saw Jesus work miracles, such as calming a storm, turning water into wine and helping to make sick people well with a touch of his hand. Followers began to believe that Jesus had God's power to heal people. Many adults and children enjoyed listening to Jesus. He told them stories and helped people to understand more about God's love and forgiveness. However, some people did not like Jesus' teaching and preaching, and they wanted to stop him, so they took him away and left him to die on a cross.

Jesus' body was carefully laid to rest in a cave and a stone door was rolled shut. A couple of days later some women went to the cave, but to their amazement the heavy stone door was open and the cave was empty. Jesus had gone!

Then one of the women saw Jesus in a garden nearby. Some of Jesus' closest friends said that they had also seen Jesus! For forty days after that, more people said that they had seen Jesus. They said that Jesus had told them to spread the good news. The people remembered all the good things Jesus had told them about, and they passed his teachings and stories on to others all around the world. This continued for year after year, and it is why he is still remembered and loved today.

Jenni Tavener

Tippity, tappity, knock

(Sung to the tune of 'Hickory, Dickory, Dock')

Tippity, tappity, knock, *(Mime tapping a boiled egg.)*
The egg begins to rock, *(Sway hands from side to side.)*
It crashes down, *(Clap hands.)*
And rolls around, *(Spin arms.)*
The yolk drips out, slip, slop! *(Run fingers down face.)*

Jenni Tavener

Sun come out

(Sung to the tune of 'Rain, Rain, Go Away')

Ready, steady, clap and say, *(Clap hands.)*
Sun come out for Easter Day. *(Cup hands in front of mouth as if calling.)*
Ready, steady, clap and say, *(Repeat first action.)*
Easter time is here, hurray! *(Repeat second action.)*

Jenni Tavener

This poor old Easter egg!

(Sung to the tune of 'The Grand Old Duke of York')

Oh, this poor old Easter egg, *(Draw an egg shape in the air.)*
It's in ten thousand bits, *(Flash ten fingers several times.)*
It's lying here, it's lying there, it's lying everywhere! *(Point to floor.)*
And when it broke it smashed, *(Clap hands or slap thighs.)*
And when it smashed it broke, *(As above.)*
And now it's in ten thousand bits, and lying everywhere! *(Point to floor.)*

Jenni Tavener

Five Easter chicks

(Sung to the tune of 'Five Little Ducks')

Five Easter chicks went searching one day,
For an Easter egg to give away.
They found an egg that was big and fat,
But only four Easter chicks helped carry it back!
Four Easter chicks...
Three Easter chicks...
Two Easter chicks...
One Easter chick went searching one day,
For an Easter egg to give away.
He found an egg that was big and fat,
But no Easter chicks helped carry it back!

Jenni Tavener

Hip, hop, wriggle

(Sung to the tune of 'In and Out the Dusty Bluebells')

In and out jumps the Easter bunny,
In and out jumps the Easter bunny,
In and out jumps the Easter bunny,
Let's all jump together.
Hip, hop, hip, hop, wriggle my tail,
Hip, hop, hip, hop, wriggle my tail,
Hip, hop, hip, hop, wriggle my tail,
Let's all jump together.

Jenni Tavener

EASTER GIFT BAG

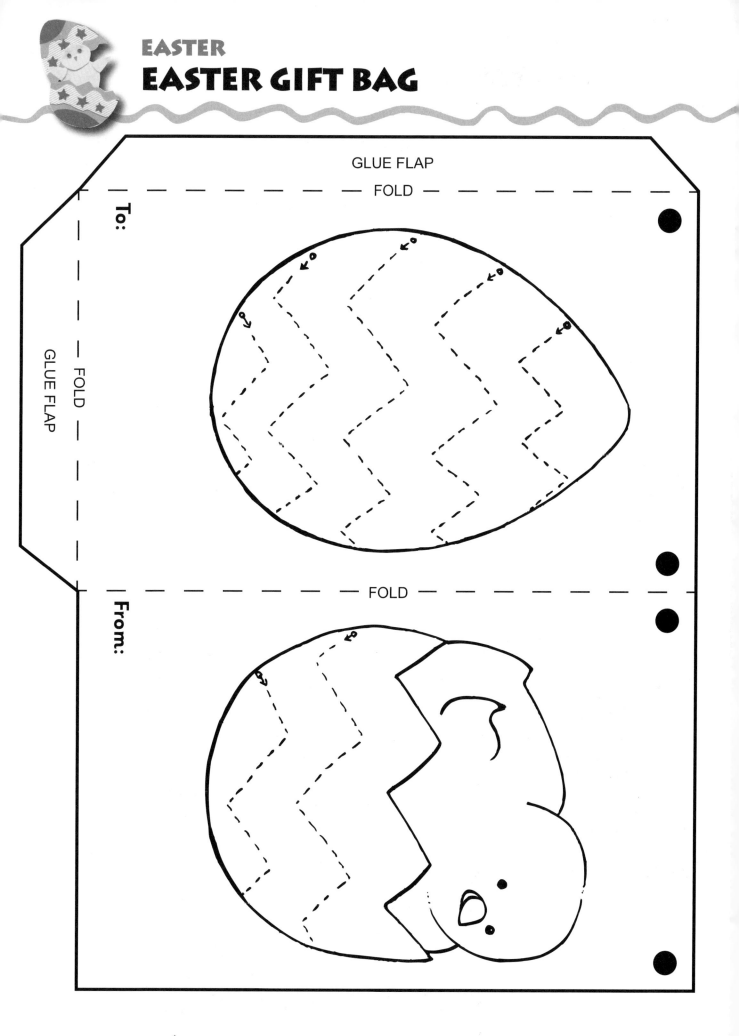

GLUE FLAP

— FOLD —

To:

FOLD
GLUE FLAP

— FOLD —

From:

— FOLD —

EASTER
HATCHING OUT

● Cut around the dotted lines and glue the circles back to back.

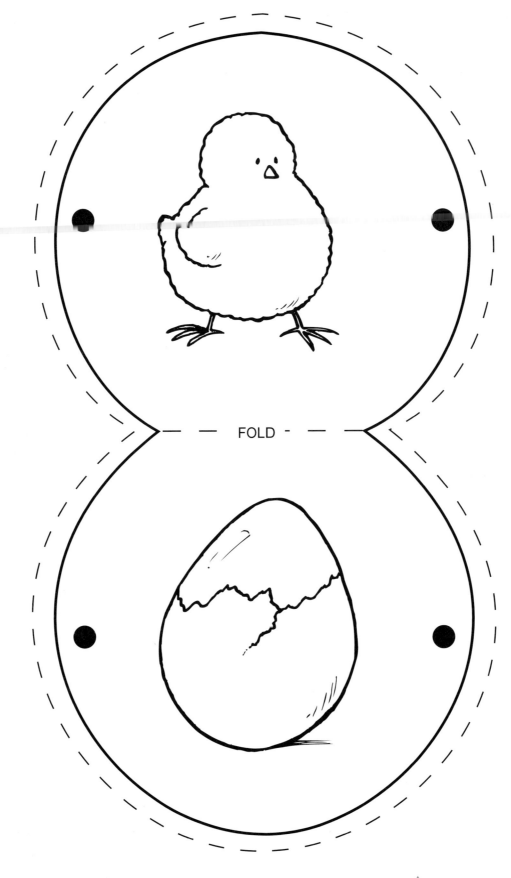

FOLD

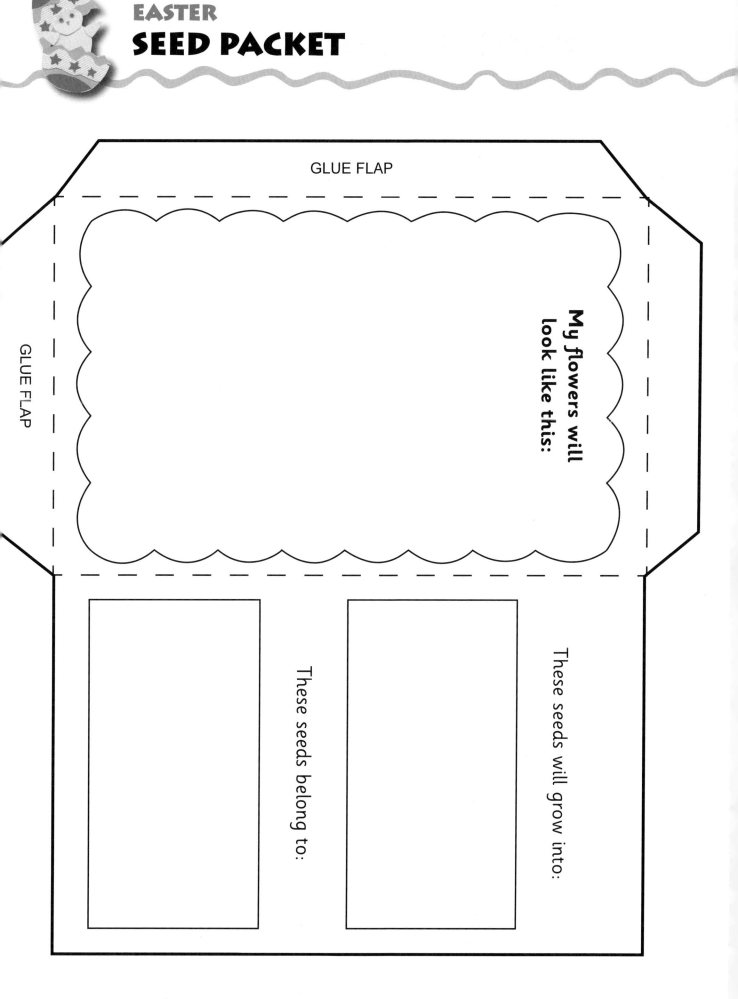

GLUE FLAP

GLUE FLAP

My flowers will look like this:

These seeds belong to:

These seeds will grow into:

RESOURCES

Story and picture books

Christmas
Spot's First Christmas by Eric Hill (Puffin Books)
Mr Christmas by Roger Hargreaves (Egmont Books)
Mog's Christmas by Judith Kerr (Collins)
Jingle Bells by Nick Butterworth (Collins)
Careful Santa by Julie Sykes (Little Tiger Press)
Christmas Activity Book by Catherine Bruzzone and Clare Beaton (B. Small Publishing)
The Jolly Christmas Postman by Janet and Allan Ahlberg (Heinemann)

Easter
Spot's First Easter by Eric Hill (Puffin Books)
Daisy and the Egg by Jane Simmons (Orchard Books)
The Runaway Bunny by Margaret Wise Brown (Picture Lions)
The Golden Egg by A J Wood (Templar)
Eggday by Joyce Dunbar and Jane Cabrera (David & Charles Children's Books)
Little Lamb by Piers Harper (Macmillan Children's Books)

Equipment

Christmas
Christmas Foam Stamps available from Philip and Tacey (North Way, Andover, Hants SP10 5BA, tel: 01264-332171)
Baby Jesus board book and play puzzle (Ladybird Books)

Easter
Spring Shapes sponge painting available from NES Arnold (Findel House, Excelsior Road, Ashby Park, Ashby de la Zouch, Leicestershire LE65 1NG, tel: 0845-120 4525)

Religious stories retold

Christmas
The Christmas Story retold by Lois Rock (Lion Publishing)
Stories Jesus Told – Favourite Stories from The Bible by Nick Butterworth and Mick Inkpen (Marshall Pickering)
The Story of Christmas by Vivian French (Walker Books)
The Usborne Children's Bible retold by Heather Amery (*Usborne Bible Tales*, Usborne Publishing)

Easter
The Easter Story retold by Heather Amery (*Usborne Bible Tales*, Usborne Publishing)
The Easter Story retold by Lois Rock (Lion Publishing)
Stories Jesus Told – The Lost Sheep by Nick Butterworth and Mick Inkpen (Marshall Pickering)

Poetry and prayer books

Thank you prayers by Sophie Piper (Lion Publishing)
Out and About by Shirley Hughes (Walker Books)

Song books

Spring Tinderbox compiled by Chris Deshpande and Julia Eccleshare (A & C Black)
The Usborne Book of Christmas Carols illustrated by Stephen Cartwright (Usborne Publishing)